MATA HARI

A Life From Beginning to End

Copyright © 2019 by Hourly History.

All rights reserved.

Table of Contents

Introduction
Tumultuous Childhood
A Wife and Mother
The Night of Horror
Becoming Mata Hari
Dance Rivals
Outbreak of World War I
Code Name H21
Becoming a Spy
Betrayal
The Trial and Execution of Mata Hari
Conclusion

Introduction

Margaretha Zelle, Gretha MacLeod, Madame Rousseau, the woman known as Mata Hari went by many different names. Born in 1876 in a small city in the Netherlands, Margaretha Zelle was a spoiled child. She was taught that the three ingredients needed for happiness were luxury, affection, and good social standing. Margaretha tried to win her happiness through marriage but chose the wrong man. When it became clear to her that no one man could give her everything she needed, her transformation began.

As Mata Hari, Margaretha could live the perfect life. Often referred to as an exotic dancer, Mata Hari was the leading experimental dance artist of her day. Never before had someone taken the ceremonial dances of an eastern country and performed them, interpretively and nearly nude, on the most prestigious stages in Europe. When she wasn't dancing, Mata Hari was a professional courtier. Enjoying liaisons with some of the most powerful men in Europe, Mata Hari made no apologies for her lifestyle. She was not ashamed. When those same powerful men turned on each other and went to war, they unanimously turned against Mata Hari and the pre-war decadence she represented. Now Mata Hari was a spy.

This story is familiar. But what about Mata Hari's life before the stage? Her marriage and children and her years in Indonesia—how did Mata Hari go from an unknown Dutch divorcee to Europe's most famous and notorious woman? By the time of her death, Mata Hari was no longer dancing, but she was resolutely in love. Who was this man who might have been her last-minute salvation? As Mata Hari herself bent the truth to suit her liking, the story of this woman's life will always be elusive. This is an attempt to capture at least some of it.

Chapter One

Tumultuous Childhood

"I wanted to live like a colorful butterfly in the sun."

—Mata Hari

Margaretha "Margreet" Zelle was born on August 7, 1876 in Leeuwarden, Netherlands. As the eldest child and only girl in the family, Margaretha was adored from the moment she opened her eyes. Her father, Adam Zelle, was particularly fond of his daughter and lavished her with gifts and affection. To Adam, Margaretha was incredibly precious and deserved every luxury he could possibly give her. And he could give her a lot.

Adam owned a hat shop and had made such good investments in the oil industry that he had become quite wealthy. Status was important to him, and his vanity and pretentious nature lent him the nickname "the Baron" around town. True to form, Adam married above his social class. When he married Antje van der Meulen, she was 31 years old, already undesirably old for matrimony, but her social standing was much higher than his. Adam was willing to put social mobility before love when it came to marriage. It's unclear whether Antje felt the same.

Margaretha was Adam's most attractive accessory, and he made sure she knew it. Adam purchased flamboyant dresses for his daughter to wear at her exclusive private school, and on her sixth birthday he gave her the extravagant gift of her own goat-drawn carriage. The miniature phaeton was a magical gift for a child and was the talk of the town for years afterward. The Zelle family lived in a class of their own.

By 1883, when Margaretha was seven, the Zelle family moved home. Adam bought a stunning brick house on Grote Kerkstraat and hired a number of new servants. As befitting the daughter of any wealthy upper-middle-class family, Margaretha attended school to learn manners, music, handwriting, and French. The Zelle family's success was, however, short-lived. By February of 1889, Adam was bankrupt. Bad investments compounded by extravagant spending had hurt the family's finances, but it was the damage to Adam's ego that could not be repaired. Adam left for the Hague to find work, and his family was forced into a subsistence lifestyle in a cramped apartment in an unfashionable part of town.

Margaretha had her thirteenth birthday soon after her father's departure. There were no gifts that year, no astonishing goat-drawn carriage for young Margaretha. She was groomed to be the ultimate daddy's girl, and Adam's departure was shocking desertion. Adam returned after ten months, but things would never be the same again for the Zelle family. Adam and Antje's marriage disintegrated under the financial stress, and the couple were soon divorced. To be divorced in late nineteenth-century Friesland was scandalous. Couples separated all the time but to divorce was disgraceful. Adam moved to

Amsterdam and was remarried within a few years. Antje remained in Leeuwarden where she did her best to keep her family alive albeit in grinding poverty.

In May 1891, Antje suddenly died. The cause of death is not known; Antje was only 49 years old. Adam remained in Amsterdam, and the Zelle children were cared for by neighbors until the family figured out something more permanent. Margaretha was almost 15 years old when she was sent to live with her uncle Mr. Visser in the small town of Sneek. This was a second betrayal by her father, who had taken his twin sons to live with him in Amsterdam. Johannes, the older son, was sent to live with his mother's family in Franeker.

Margaretha, five feet ten inches (178 cm) tall with dark hair, olive skin, and striking looks, stood out in the small conservative town of Sneek. Visser was worried that Margaretha was going to be a financial burden on him for years to come and hoped to marry her off as soon as possible. But Margaretha had no dowry, and the Zelle name had been disgraced across the region. Margaretha had been trained in the feminine arts of music, languages, and art, but she had no practical skills to speak of and domestic service was unthinkable. There was only one solution. She would become a teacher.

Visser sent Margaretha to Leiden school where she was to live with the headmaster and train to be a kindergarten teacher. The story of what happened next is predictable. The headteacher of the school fell in love with Margaretha and pursued a relationship with her. She was 16 years old. When Visser found out about the relationship, he had Margaretha sent back to Sneek in shame. Margaretha was perceived to be the seducer, despite the fact that the headteacher was 51 years old and in a position of authority.

At age 17, Margaretha was passed into the care of another set of estranged relatives, this time in the Hague. She still had no real prospects and no dowry for marriage, but the Hague was an exciting place to be. A cosmopolitan city that was and still is the seat of parliament, the Hague of the late nineteenth century was also alive with soldiers on leave.

Chapter Two

A Wife and Mother

"Officer on home leave from Dutch East Indies would like to meet a girl of pleasant character—object matrimony."

—Rudolf MacLeod's newspaper advert for a wife

The man who would become Margaretha's first and only husband was named Rudolf MacLeod. Rudolf was born on March 1, 1856, making him 20 years older than Margaretha, and was a captain in the Dutch Colonial Army. When the pair first met in 1895, Rudolf had lived and fought in the Dutch East Indies for the same number of years Margaretha had been alive.

Rudolf and Margaretha did not meet by accident. In January of 1894, Rudolf was granted two years of home leave due to ill health. He was not well enough to travel until later in the year, and by August 1894 he was recuperating in Amsterdam at the home of his sister, Louise. A man used to the thrill of warfare and the privileges of being a Dutchman in the Dutch East Indies, Rudolf was soon bored of his convalescence. A friend of Rudolf's decided that what he needed was a wife and placed an advert in the newspaper. The ad read: "Officer on home leave from Dutch East Indies would like to meet a girl of pleasant character—object matrimony."

A number of women replied to Rudolf's advert, but only one had the clever idea of including a photograph, Margaretha Zelle. Margaretha and Rudolf exchanged letters that quickly grew amorous. Margaretha called Rudolf "Johnnie," a family nickname, and he called her "Gretha." Before they had even met in person, Margaretha began signing her letters, "your little wifey."

The more Margaretha learned of Rudolf, the more she liked him. Rudolf was born into a prominent Scottish family with a proud military and aristocratic heritage. Several generations of the men in his family were military officers while his mother was a baroness whose fortune was lost before she was born. Margaretha also had a soft spot for military men. In an interview given later in her life she said, "Yes, I have had many lovers, but it is the beautiful soldiers, brave, always ready for battle and, while waiting, always sweet and gallant. For me, the officer forms a race apart. I have never loved any but officers."

If Margaretha was romantic later in life, she was starry-eyed in her youth. In Rudolf, she saw a hero—her ticket out of a life of boredom with ungenerous relatives, unable to support herself. Rudolf would be her support, her sweet and gallant officer who would make life an adventure. But Margaretha knew nothing of the realities of war or the realities of her fiancé's character. Rudolf was not gallant at all; he was in a great deal of debt and in poor health, with symptoms that suggested he had venereal disease.

Although Margaretha was aware Rudolf was on sick leave from the military and that his health was fragile, she knew nothing of his history. Blissfully ignorant, she assumed he would soon be back to full strength. Margaretha didn't know that disease was rampant amongst the Dutch military. During the rainy season in the Dutch East Indies, around 60 percent of soldier deaths could be attributed to illness rather than injury. Diseases included malaria, cholera, dysentery, and syphilis, none of which could be cured. Margaretha had neither the temperament nor the desire to be a nursemaid. Nor did she have any intention of being the good stay-at-home wife Rudolf wanted her to be.

Nevertheless, Margaretha and Rudolf were married at Amsterdam City Hall on July 11, 1895. After a lavish honeymoon in the German spa town of Wiesbaden, the pair returned to the Netherlands to live with Louise, Rudolf's sister. The marriage deteriorated immediately. Rudolf did not have the income his military standing and social background suggested. During his sick leave, he was on part pay and most of that was swallowed up by the debt he had built up through living way beyond his means. Margaretha had no talent for frugality, and her taste for luxury added to Rudolf's financial woes. Rudolf continued with his heavy drinking and womanizing, just as he had done as a bachelor, and Margaretha spent lavishly and flirted with other men at every opportunity. The spoiled young woman and the arrogant old soldier were not a match made in heaven.

A year into their marriage, the pair were still living with Louise when Margaretha became pregnant. Rudolf's leave was extended as it was inadvisable for a pregnant woman to travel to the Dutch East Indies. Margaretha gave birth to a baby boy she named Norman-John on January 30, 1897. Rudolf's lifestyle did not change after the birth of his son, and he continued to spend most of his evenings out drinking and spending money on women who were not his wife. Home alone with her baby, Margaretha was miserable. So when it was time to finally start a new life in the Dutch East Indies, she was excited. The MacLeods set sail on the S.S. *Prinses Amalia* on May 1, 1897. Margaretha had no idea what life in the colonies was like, but she figured it had to be better than the life she had in Amsterdam.

Chapter Three

The Night of Horror

"That God should deliver me from this creature! I hope with all my heart. Amen!"

—Rudolf MacLeod

Margaretha's arrival in the Dutch East Indies was like a rebirth. For her, who had never left the Netherlands, the Indies were a strange land of beauty and intrigue. The heat of the Indies, the lush vegetation, the food, the people—Margaretha drank it in as though she was parched. And she was. The strict moral codes, dull weather, and ennui of the Netherlands never suited her. In the Indies, Margaretha could find herself.

Margaretha's metamorphosis may have been a happy experience had it not been for her disastrously unhappy marriage. In the Indies, she had hoped that her rise in status would bring with it greater freedoms. In reality, the opposite was true. At only 20 years old, Margaretha was the wife of an important man who expected her to run the household with absolute seriousness.

Although a captain's wife, Margaretha was not immune to local gossip. The subject of the whispers going on behind her back was her race. Margaretha's skin tone was darker than the average white Dutch person. Once transformed into Mata Hari, the exotic dancer from the east, her coloring was a huge advantage and allowed her to pass herself off as non-European. But in Dutch East Indies, where officers regularly had long-term relationships with Indonesian women, Margaretha's skin color left her subject to slurs.

On May 2, 1898, Margaretha gave birth to her second child, a girl named Louise Jeanne. The little girl became known as "Non," a Javanese nickname meaning "little miss." After Non's birth, the tension between Margaretha and Rudolf intensified. Rudolf accused his wife of infidelity which was likely hypocritical as it was common for European men in the Indies to have *nyais*, Indonesian mistresses. Life in the Indies soon wore Margaretha down, and by early 1899 she had had enough. Writing to her father she said, "No, I have no more beautiful illusions about the Indies because if you really look at it, it is not a nice country . . . If I could I would come back tomorrow."

In March of 1899, Rudolf was promoted and sent to serve in Medan. There were far fewer Europeans in Medan than in Tumpang, where the MacLeod family had been living. As a result, racial barriers were even more aggressively enforced, on the surface at least. Rudolf went ahead to Medan to get a house ready for his young family's arrival and almost certainly spent time with a nyai while there. Money was incredibly tight, and Rudolf hardy sent anything for Margaretha and the children to live on while they waited for his summons. By the time the family was reunited in Medan, Margaretha and Rudolf could barely stand to look at each other.

There was another issue. Rudolf was obsessed with his children's health and didn't seem to trust Margaretha to take care of them. It's a strong possibility that Rudolf's syphilis was at the heart of the newlyweds' hatred for each other. If Rudolf passed his disease on to Margaretha early in their marriage, their two children would likely be sufferers too. It was a terrible situation for everyone.

Then on June 27, 1899, the unthinkable happened. Both of the MacLeod children became dangerously ill. The children were both vomiting, bringing up black liquid and writhing in pain. Norman, who was two years and five months old at the time, sank into unconsciousness. He died before a doctor could be summoned. Non gradually recovered from her illness, but the loss of Norman destroyed what was left of the MacLeod family.

Vicious rumors circulated about the cause of Norman's death. Whispers that Norman's *babu*, his Indonesian nurse, had poisoned him in an act of revenge against Rudolf gained credence through repetition. A similar story blaming the cook circulated. No autopsy was performed on Norman, but the most convincing theory holds that he died of mercury poisoning. The mercury was administered by a doctor attempting to cure Norman of congenital syphilis. A dose of mercuric chloride was the standard treatment of the time. It was incredibly easy to overdose when administering this toxic mixture to small children.

Whatever the exact cause of Norman's death, Rudolf was convinced that it was Margaretha's fault, and she was convinced it was his. Rudolf was demoted soon after

Norman's death, and the MacLeods moved to Banjoe Biroe, a small village near Sumatra. Here, Margaretha and Rudolf's hatred for each other descended into emotional and physical abuse. Rudolf was so jealous of the attention his wife received from other men that he admitted in letters that he wanted to kill her.

Rudolf offered Margaretha a divorce, but she refused for financial reasons and endured his anger. The pair began to wish for each other's early death. When Margaretha become dangerously ill with typhoid, Rudolf wrote to his sister, Louise, "That God should deliver me from this creature! I hope with all my heart. Amen!" Something had to give.

By May of 1901, Margaretha was writing to her father saying that she feared for her life. She revealed the terrible abuse Rudolf inflicted on her in these letters, including being beaten with a cat-o'-nine-tails and threatened with a loaded gun. In March of 1902, Rudolf, Gretha, and their daughter Jeanne returned to Amsterdam in a last-ditch attempt to save their marriage. The attempt failed, and in August of the same year, Rudolf abducted Non and disappeared. Margaretha convinced Rudolf to bring Non back and filed for divorce.

On August 30, 1902, the court agreed that reconciliation between the ill-matched and hate-filled pair was impossible. Legal separation was granted. Margaretha tried to take care of Non herself with no financial help from Rudolf, but it proved impossible. After a short and desperate reunion, Margaretha recognized that she had no cards left in her pack. With no other option available to her, she agreed Non should stay with Rudolf and she should leave for good. The period of Margaretha's life spent as a wife and a mother was officially over.

Chapter Four

Becoming Mata Hari

"I thought all women who ran away from their husbands went to Paris."

—Mata Hari

A journalist once asked Margaretha why she chose Paris as her new home in 1903. "I don't know. I thought all women who ran away from their husbands went to Paris," she said. In Paris, Margaretha had no dependents, but she also had no one she could depend on. To support herself, she sought work as a model. Margaretha may have also tried her hand at acting but found the most dependable way to put food on the table and clothes on her back was to please men for money.

In the spring of 1904, Margaretha took a job with an equestrian circus. This job didn't last long, but it stirred her love for the stage. Margaretha knew she wanted a career in performance—she just needed to figure out what kind. Before long, she had chosen the medium of dance as her calling and put together a number of what she called "sacred dances." Margaretha understood that to be successful, she had to set herself apart from every other young dancer in Paris. It was time for a brand new identity.

Basing her movements on traditional Indonesian dance, Margaretha developed a seductive dancing style that relied on nudity and the allure of the exotic. Wearing costumes inspired by ancient Javanese court dancers, Margaretha moved in slow, undulating movements as she gently shed her loosely fitting veils. Her dancing style escaped accusations of impropriety by claiming to be holy, an act of worship. Her dance wasn't pornography, she claimed; it was art.

The mythology of Mata Hari began to take shape. Margaretha adopted the name Lady MacLeod and claimed to be a widow. Her first performances were private and took place in the home of Madame Kireevsky, a society hostess who acted as a patron of the arts. From here, Margaretha's career took on a life of its own. She made her public debut in a performance for 600 members of the Parisian elite at the Musée Guimet on March 13, 1905. At this performance, she first unveiled her stage name, Mata Hari, meaning "sun" (literally "eye of the day") in Malay.

Between dances, Mata Hari explained the meaning of her performance. She said, "My dance is a sacred poem in which each movement is a word and whose every word is underlined by music. The temple in which I dance can be vague or faithfully reproduced, as here today. For I am the temple." The audience was mesmerized.

The timing was right. European high society's obsession with the art and culture of the east was at its peak. And in Paris, the behaviors of the pleasure-seeking *demi-monde* were filtering into the mainstream.

Everywhere you looked, glamor, excess, and sensuality were on display.

In 1905 alone, Mata Hari danced in more than 30 public and private performances. Some of these performances were given in front of sold-out audiences at famous theatres like the Trocadero. Some were in the homes of patrons, like the banker Baron Henri de Rothschild. It didn't take long for news of Mata Hari's success to appear in the press. Speculation about Mata Hari's true identity dominated articles written about her, and in interviews she spun webs of lies to intensify her own mystique. But she couldn't hide her identity for long. In a publication named *Today's Woman*, Mata Hari was outed as Mrs. MacLeod.

Predictably, Rudolf was enraged. It was humiliating enough to be deserted by your wife. For your wife to go on to be Europe's most celebrated sex symbol was unbearable. Rudolf decided to seek a divorce on the grounds of her immoral behavior, indecency, and adultery. Armed with nude photographs of Mata Hari, taken during her performances, Rudolf's attorney argued for full custody of Non. Knowing she couldn't fight Rudolf's claims of indecency, Mata Hari acquiesced. The divorce was granted in April of 1906, and Mata Hari lost all contact with her daughter.

Back in Paris, Mata Hari's career was going from strength to strength. With Gabriel Astruc working as her manager, she secured a performance at the Olympia Theatre in Paris, for which she earned the huge sum of 10,000 francs. Next Mata Hari went to Madrid where she mesmerized Spanish audiences and made the acquaintance of Jules Cambon, the French ambassador in Madrid. Cambon was head over heels for Mata Hari and hosted a lavish reception for her to introduce her to all his official friends. This relationship would be important later in Mata Hari's life.

In February 1906, Mata Hari danced in the opera *Le Roi de Lahore* in Monte Carlo. This was one of Mata Hari's most important and critically acclaimed performances. *Le Roi* was a much-loved opera. Mata Hari's role gave her a dose of stage legitimacy and gained her yet more admiring lovers, including Jules Massanet, *Le Roi*'s composer and a leading musician of the day.

Mata Hari's life as a courtesan is harder to keep track of than her career—not because Mata Hari was secretive about her lovers. On the contrary, she found no conflict in being a celebrated beauty and performer and a well-known courtesan. But Mata Hari had relationships with many men in positions of power in Europe, at a time of great political unrest.

After performing in Monte Carlo, Mata Hari went to Berlin where she performed for adoring audiences. While there, she met a wealthy German lieutenant, Alfred Kiepert. Kiepert revered Mata Hari and set her up with an apartment in Berlin and accompanied her across Europe for her dancing engagements. The relationship lasted three years, and while it was not a secret, Kiepert took pains to keep Mata Hari separate from his wife. When Kiepert's wife issued an ultimatum, he broke off his relationship with Mata Hari and gave her 300,000 gold marks, the equivalent of more than $4 million today.

Chapter Five

Dance Rivals

"Isadora Duncan is dead! Long live Mata Hari!"

—*New Vienna Journal*

In the early 1900s, Mata Hari's performance style was unique. No other dancers were combining the oriental allure of the east with risqué nudity—at least not as well as Mata Hari. But there were other popular dancers. Isadora Duncan was an established dancer before Mata Hari hit the Paris scene. She was famous for dancing with bare legs and no corset, details that shocked audiences long before Mata Hari danced nude under veils. Duncan was French-American and trained as a dancer from a very young age. Known for her innovative technique that emphasized fluid, natural movement and rejected traditional ballet moves, Duncan was a true artist. She couldn't stand self-promotion and wanted nothing to do with the commercial side of her performances. In this aspect, Duncan was the opposite of Mata Hari.

In late 1906, Mata Hari performed in Vienna where she enraptured audiences and the press. The *New Vienna Journal* printed the headline, "Isadora Duncan is dead! Long live Mata Hari!" Mata Hari was thrilled and used her linguistic advantage (Duncan did not speak German) to charm critics and interviewers. It was in Vienna that a writer described Mata Hari as "slender and tall, with the flexible grace of a wild animal and blue-black hair . . . a small face that makes a strange foreign impression. Forehead and nose are of classical shape – as if copied from antiquity. Black long lashes throw a shadow on her eyes, and the eyebrows are so finely and gracefully bent that it seems as if they were drawn by an artist."

Another dancer often mentioned in the same breath as Mata Hari was Maud Allan. Allan's performance style was closer to Mata Hari's than Duncan's. She became known for her performances playing Salome, dressed in a pseudo-oriental garb not unlike Mata Hari's and dancing seductively in breastplates and a headdress. Mata Hari called Allan out in the press, thanking her for honoring her with imitation but reminding everyone of the clear difference between the two dancers. Allan was an imitator, but Mata Hari was the real thing, "born in Java in the midst of tropical vegetation." Mata Hari had introduced herself to her first audience in Paris with a story of Javanese heritage—a story which she stuck to. Only Mata Hari could impart the true religious significance of the dances she solemnly performed.

In 1908, Mata Hari was at the peak of her career, a shining star excelling in both of her arts: dance and seduction. Inspired by Mata Hari's success, young dancers flooded the music-hall stages of Europe with their own interpretation of oriental dance. Exotic and revealing costumes became the norm, and audiences were becoming familiar with the music and stage production Mata Hari had introduced. Now in her early thirties, Mata Hari knew that to ensure her star continued to rise, she would have to bring something new to the stage.

Perhaps as a jab at Maud Allan, Mata Hari campaigned for the part of Salome in Richard Strauss's opera. Allan had danced in Oscar Wilde's scandalous version of the tale, and Mata Hari no doubt wanted to show how it should be done. But Strauss didn't want her for the part. The rejection was a blow. Mata Hari was not used to being denied the thing she wanted. She sought solace in a new lover, stockbroker Xavier Rousseau.

Much more than a brief flirtation, Mata Hari's relationship with Xavier Rousseau became something close to a marriage. Rousseau set up his lover in a country chateau near Tours where she was referred to as Madame Rousseau. Rousseau stayed with Mata Hari every weekend, and the rest of the time she lived like French aristocracy; she rode horses, attended races, and had staff who tended to her every whim. With no imperative to earn money herself, Mata Hari rarely danced, content it seemed to bow out of the war of the tights, victorious.

In 1911, Mata Hari and Rousseau moved to a mansion in Neuilly-sur-Seine and resumed their lavish life. Yet despite being a stockbroker, Rousseau either had no head for figures or felt he had no choice but to keep Mata Hari in the state of excess to which she was accustomed. Either way, by 1912, he was bankrupt. Rousseau not only squandered his own fortune and returned to his wife a ruined man, but he also lost Mata Hari's private wealth. According to Mata Hari, she lost up to 200,000 francs, including everything she had left from Kiepert's parting gift, when Rousseau left her. She had no choice but to return to the stage.

In 1911, Mata Hari danced in La Scala in Milan in Gluck's opera, *Armide*. At the same theatre, she danced in Marenco's ballet *Bacco e Gambrinus*. Mata Hari was not a ballerina and yet critics were impressed with her performance, and she reclaimed her status as Europe's premier dancer. However, no performance in a short-run opera or ballet would be enough to finance Mata Hari's luxurious lifestyle. With Rousseau back at home with his wife, Mata Hari set about finding another wealthy man. She wrote to her agent to ask whether he knew "anyone who would be interested in the protection of artists, like a capitalist who would like to make an investment?"

Chapter Six
Outbreak of World War I

"Deutschland über alles! (Germany above all!)"

—Patriotic song sung by German soldiers during World War I

In 1913, Mata Hari turned 37 years old. Sensing that her career as a dancer had reached its zenith, she did what she could to stay in the public eye. Still revered by the European public and press, she gave garden parties for her influential friends, during which she effectively rented out her mansion in Neuilly for parties and acted as hostess. At her private parties, Mata Hari performed with an Indian orchestra playing traditional instruments. This orchestra was led by Inayat Khan, a master musician.

Yet Mata Hari could not replicate her earlier success. In fact, she began to experience her first rejections from the dance establishment. When she traveled to Monte Carlos in 1913 to meet with the head of the Ballets Russes, the ballet's famous costume designer Leon Bakst asked to see Mata Hari naked to begin preparations for her costume. On examining her unclothed body, Leon remarked that her figure was too matronly for her to dance ballet. Humiliated, Mata Hari left.

Before the year reached its end, Mata Hari was performing at venues previously beneath her. Alongside private parties, she performed in musical comedy and at the Folies Bergère. To supplement her dancing income, she also supposedly frequented *maisons de rendez-vouz*, high-class brothels.

Around this time, Mata Hari began thinking about Non. It had been years since she had seen her daughter, and she was concerned about her education and home life. Rudolf MacLeod's second wife had divorced him, leaving Non without a mother figure. Mata Hari wanted Non to join her in Paris, although it's not clear how this arrangement would work. Non was a teenager attending school and couldn't slip easily into Mata Hari's lifestyle. Unfazed by these challenges, Mata Hari was so adamant she wanted Non back in her life that she sent her loyal maid Anna to Holland to kidnap Non after school. However, Rudolf was there waiting, foiling his ex-wife's plan. Mata Hari gave up, and mother and daughter were never reunited.

It was becoming more and more difficult for Mata Hari to survive in Paris, and in 1914, she returned to Berlin. She announced that she was quitting dance forever and that she was researching ancient Egyptian culture to create a new dance; contradiction was never an issue for Mata Hari. Berlin had some of the world's best collections of Egyptian antiquities so research could explain her move. Once settled in Berlin, she was offered a lucrative contract to dance at the Metropol Theatre. The contract was for six months, for which Mata Hari would be paid a salary of 48,000 francs. This sum could keep Mata Hari in her exuberant lifestyle. While in Berlin, she also checked in on an old flame. In 1914, Mata Hari and Alfred Kiepert resumed their affair.

Mata Hari's run at the Metropol wasn't due to begin until September of 1914. She intended to spend months leading up to it as she always had, in lavish luxury, being received in high society on the arm of her lover. But something had changed in Berlin, as it had across most of Europe. The *Belle Époque*—or the Beautiful Era—that defined the turn of the century as a high point in arts, science, and society was at an end. A dark shadow was creeping over Europe bringing with it a conservative, nationalistic sense of urgency. Women who lived as Mata Hari did were no longer welcome in polite society.

At the outbreak of the First World War, Mata Hari had a number of lovers. Among them was Mr. Griebel, a chief of police. In late July 1914, Mata Hari was dining with Griebel in the private room of a fashionable restaurant when a riot broke out. Austria had invaded Serbia a few days before, and the city was tense with anticipation. The tension broke out in a violent demonstration in front of the emperor's palace with demonstrators chanting, "Deutschland über alles! (Germany above all!)"

Mata Hari couldn't ignore the unrest any longer. She knew her beautiful home and treasured belongings back in France were at risk as she was not a French citizen. If only she could return to Paris, she had a chance of stopping the French authorities from seizing her property.

A few days after the riot, Germany declared war on Russia and France. Now Mata Hari was in serious trouble. Her accounts were frozen in Germany, and her costumier seized her jewelry and furs. As a longtime resident of France, Mata Hari was not welcome in Germany, nor could she return to France as she was not a citizen. Although she had many powerful friends in high places in both Germany and France, none would risk being seen to help a foreigner. It was a dilemma that would be Mata Hari's undoing.

Chapter Seven

Code Name H21

"Certainly this life suits me. I can satisfy all my caprices; tonight I dine with Count A and tomorrow with Duke B. If I don't have to dance, I make a trip with Marquis C. I avoid serious liaisons."

—Mata Hari

As in Indonesia, Mata Hari's dark coloring worked against her. The striking features and dark skin and hair that had helped Mata Hari sell herself as a Javanese court dancer were now a liability. Police stopped her on the street and demanded that she produce her Dutch passport to prove her nationality. Convinced she was Russian, police transported her to the police station on a number of occasions.

Mata Hari was determined to escape Germany. She boarded a train to Switzerland on August 6, 1914 with an extensive set of luggage but hardly a franc in her purse. It seems she didn't have the appropriate documentation to prove her neutral Dutch citizenship, or if she did, the authorities simply wouldn't accept it. Mata Hari was thrown off the train to Switzerland somewhere in Germany and forced to take another train back to Berlin, without her luggage.

Back at her hotel in Berlin, Mata Hari plotted what to do next. She had to travel to Frankfurt to get a new Dutch passport, then she would go directly to Amsterdam. But before she started her journey, there were a few things to attend to. First, she needed money. Mata Hari quickly made the acquaintance of a Dutch businessman who was sympathetic to his fellow Dutchwoman and offered to pay her fare to Amsterdam. Next, Mata Hari had her hair dyed in an attempt to conceal her identity and perhaps her age. Her new Dutch passport listed her age as 38, her height as 5 ft 11, and her hair color as blonde.

Mata Hari successfully returned to Holland in late 1914. She moved into a house in the Hague and somehow convinced a contractor to make extensive renovations with no money to pay him. The contractors accepted her request to pay nothing for two years from the day she moved in. With no way to support herself and nothing to show for her long and successful career, Mata Hari made money the only way she could—by being a mistress to wealthy men. She reignited her affair with Baron Edouard Willem van der Capellan, a colonel in the Dutch military.

Van der Capellan covered Mata Hari's expenses, including her maid Anna's salary, but she soon ran up debts. Hounded by creditors and quickly bored with life in the Hague, Mata Hari looked for distractions. There was no fun to be had anymore with no fuel, little food, and definitely no glamor in Holland during the First World War. Then, in the autumn of 1915, the German consul in Amsterdam, Karl Kroemer, arrived.

Kroemer tried to recruit Mata Hari as a spy for Germany. He offered her the sum of 20,000 francs to pass information to the German government using invisible ink. Her code name would be H21. Mata Hari refused—not on moral grounds but on financial ones. The sum offered was not high enough. Nevertheless, Mata Hari took the money with, she claimed, no intention of ever helping the Germans. The Germans had mistreated her when war broke out—they had seized her furs, jewelry, and money, and it was this personal slight that drove her actions, not any political allegiance. Mata Hari took care of herself, and to do this she took money from men when it was offered to her. As far as Mata Hari was concerned, this exchange with Karl Kroemer was nothing out of the ordinary.

Mata Hari couldn't settle in the Hague. Life was too sedentary, too dull. In December of 1915, she danced with the French Opera at the Royal Theater. Reviews were congratulatory, but Mata Hari was forced to adjust her style to cater conservative Dutch audiences. There was no dropping of veils during her performance any longer.

After these performances, Mata Hari decided that she couldn't bear Holland any longer and had to return to Paris. While there, she thought she might reclaim her possessions from Neuilly and sell them to raise some cash. Once back in the city she adored, she couldn't leave. Mata Hari reconnected with former lovers like Henri de Marguerie, secretary to the French foreign affairs minister. She also met new lovers, like the Marquis de Beaufort, and tried to restart her career.

Now nearly 40 years old, Mata Hari was incredibly beautiful, but taking a decade-long pause was unwise for a dancer who made her name with novelty. She tried again to arrange performances with Diaghilev's Ballets Russes, but nothing came of it. Staying in Paris long-term during wartime wasn't an option, and Mata Hari knew she had to return to the Hague. With a few crates of belongings from Neuilly, she began her long journey back to her motherland. Traveling through Spain and Portugal, she left a trail of satisfied lovers behind her.

Mata Hari had left another trail behind her as she moved through Europe. Completely unbeknownst to her, she was already under investigation by the British counterespionage unit, MI5. Mata Hari had passed through the United Kingdom on her way to Paris, and at the port of Folkestone, she had been questioned by officials who found her travels suspicious. Who was this woman, dressed extravagantly in a fur-trimmed costume with matching hat, able to speak at least five languages? Mata Hari had explained the reason for her trip to Paris and that she intended to return to the Hague as soon as possible to be with her lover, Baron van der Capellan, colonel commandant in the Dutch Army. This bold admittance to being a man's mistress did not sit well with British security. A report was drafted, stating that Mata Hari, also known as Madame Zelle MacLeod, was "most unsatisfactory and should be refused permission to return to the U.K." The report recommended that Mata Hari be put under surveillance. A copy of this report was sent to French authorities, allies of the United Kingdom.

Chapter Eight

Becoming a Spy

"If you love all of France, you could render us a great service. Have you thought of it?"

—Georges Ladoux

Mata Hari returned to the Hague in early 1916 but could think of nothing but how she could return to Paris. Europe was at war, but as far as Mata Hari was concerned, it had nothing to do with her. Why shouldn't she return to the country she loved? Of course, she had no idea at this time that the British counterespionage unit was keeping a very close eye on her movements and her accounts.

According to British intelligence, Mata Hari received 15,000 francs from the German embassy in early 1916. Now they were convinced that she was a spy. When she tried to return to Paris via the U.K. in May 1916, she was denied a visa to enter. Undeterred and still unaware that this visa refusal spelled trouble, Mata Hari took a different route to Paris, via Spain. At the border between Spain and France at Hendaye, she was again interrogated. Mata Hari simply couldn't believe that she was a *persona non grata* in France, the place she felt most at home. She sent a letter to one of her lovers, Jules Cambon, now the secretary-general of the French Ministry of Foreign Affairs. But before the letter even reached Cambon, the border guards, overwhelmed by Mata Hari's self-assurance, allowed her through.

Believing all that unpleasantness was firmly behind her, Mata Hari tried to resume the glitzy lifestyle she had so adored. Living at the Grand Hotel, she did not see the devastating effect the Battle of Verdun had on the French population. Mata Hari went about her days much as she had done pre-war on a daily whirlwind tour of Paris's best dressmakers, jewelers, manicurists, florists, hairdressers, hotels, cafes, and restaurants. She also had reunions with a number of lovers, including the Marquis de Beaufort, a high-ranking Belgian officer.

We have detailed records of exactly how Mata Hari spent her days and nights in Paris around June 1916 because she was being followed by two French agents named Tarlet and Monier. It seems Mata Hari knew she was being watched, but by whom, she didn't seem to be concerned. She was used to being the center of attention. While she made attempts to lose the men who were tailing her from time to time, for the most part, she let them follow along two steps behind.

Around this time, Mata Hari met up with an old lover, Second Lieutenant Jean Hallaure, who was wounded in battle and now served at the French military intelligence agency. Hallaure spent a great deal of time with Mata Hari in July of 1916 and seemed to be completely infatuated with her. But then, in late July, Mata Hari fell in love. The object of her affection was a Russian captain named Vladimir Maslov. "Vadim," as Mata Hari called him, was in his early twenties, almost half her age. He was stationed at the western front near Mailly and had to return to his post in early August. Mata Hari's romance with Vadim was brief but intense, and she promised to meet with him soon at Vittel, near Mailly.

Mata Hari had been trying to get to Vittel, a popular spa town only a stone's throw from the western front, for a number of weeks. She was sick, she said, and needed the waters to restore her health. Since she was unable to obtain a travel permit, she tried various ways to get one, even enlisting the help of her lover, Hallaure. Hallaure promised to help Mata Hari get the documentation she required but sent her first to meet with Captain Georges Ladoux, head of the French intelligence agency. Hallaure later denied that he organized Mata Hari's meeting with Ladoux. However it came about, this meeting would change Mata Hari's life forever.

In Ladoux's office, Mata Hari was interrogated. Ladoux described the encounter in detail in his memoirs. The woman Ladoux depicts is cunning and charming and barely reacts when he accuses her outright of being a German spy. Ladoux has no evidence, he admits, but he has a vague feeling, a gut instinct that knows Mata Hari is up to no good. Mata Hari describes the first encounter between herself and Ladoux quite differently. Still intent on visiting Vittel to take the waters, she agrees to Ladoux's questioning in the hope of being awarded a travel permit at the end of it. Her account has Ladoux asking, "If you love all of France, you could render us a great service. Have you thought of it?" She replies, "Yes and no, but this is not the sort of thing for which one offers oneself." Mata Hari was not offering herself, rather Ladoux was forcing her into a role for which she was unfit. She was intelligent and cunning enough, yes, but she was also one of the most famous women in Europe.

If Mata Hari was not a spy before she entered Ladoux's office, she certainly was by the time she left.

Chapter Nine

Betrayal

"Yes, I have had many lovers, but it is the beautiful soldiers, brave, always ready for battle and, while waiting, always sweet and gallant. For me, the officer forms a race apart. I have never loved any but officers."

—Mata Hari

Following her recruitment by Ladoux, Mata Hari went back to her life as normal; she dined with officers, visited the pharmacy and hairdressers, and continued to pester officials for her permit to visit Vittel. She also continued to spend time with Hallaure from the Ministry of War.

Eventually, possibly with some pushing from one of her lovers, the secretary of the Ministry of Foreign Affairs, Mata Hari left for Vittel by train on September 1, 1916. Before she left, she called at the Russian embassy to inquire about Vadim's wellbeing. She hadn't heard from him in weeks because all of his communications had been intercepted by Ladoux. On September 3, Mata Hari and Vadim were reunited at the Grand Hotel in Vittel. He was injured, having been exposed to phosgene gas, and had lost the vision in one eye. There was a chance Vadim would lose his sight entirely.

The pair spent a few days together in Vittel and had a portrait taken to commemorate it. Mata Hari wrote on the back, "Vittel 1916—In memory of some of the most beautiful days of my life, spent with my Vadime whom I love above everything." Should Vadim survive the war, Mata Hari had agreed to marry him. The plan was that she would ask for enough money from Ladoux that she could break it off with every man she was having an affair with, reclaim her possessions from Holland, and set up home in Paris. But Vadim was from an aristocratic family and would never agree to him marrying Mata Hari if that meant they would live in poverty. If only Mata Hari could obtain enough money that she could take care of Vadim forever, even if he lost his sight.

Mata Hari returned to Paris on September 13 and immediately contacted Ladoux. According to her, Ladoux offered her one million francs to go to Belgium, seduce the military general of the country, infiltrate the German headquarters there, and procure information that would help the French war effort. Mata Hari intended to secure the information the only way she knew how. But first, she must gather a wardrobe fit for such an important seduction. Mata Hari had no money of her own; she had creditors all over Paris, hounding her for cash. Van der Capellen back in Holland was her main source of income, but his financial gifts were slow to arrive, and so she spent a difficult month in October of 1916, alternatively pleading with Ladoux for an advance and entertaining other men for money.

On November 5, Mata Hari left Paris on her way to Holland, from which she intended to begin her seduction of the military general of Belgium. She had managed to spend a few more blissful days with Vadim before she began her first mission as a spy and had wired him 500 francs before she left. This is the only time we know of that Mata Hari gave money to a man.

But Mata Hari was no spy. When she wrote her first letter to Ladoux, asking for an advance to buy a wardrobe with which she would seduce the military general of Belgium, Mata Hari refused to use invisible ink. The letter could have been infiltrated and read by anyone. She was entirely ignorant of the methods of secret agents and was herself being spied on by French, British, and possibly German agents, waiting for her to incriminate herself.

As soon as Mata Hari set foot in England she was taken by officials to Scotland Yard. Incredibly, she attracted attention for her likeness to another suspicious woman, Clara Benedix. The agents who arrested her didn't know who Mata Hari was. She was interrogated for four days. Even after she revealed that she was engaged in a mission for French intelligence and dropped a number of names, including Ladoux's, the British remained convinced that she was a German agent. Eventually the British contacted Ladoux who admitted that he had suspected Mata Hari of working for the Germans for some time and would be glad if the British could prove her guilt. He also denied hiring her as a French agent. No-one seemed to know what to do with Mata Hari, so the British released her, forbid her from traveling on to Holland, and sent her back to Vigo, Spain.

Here, Mata Hari met with Martial Cazeaux, a Frenchman stationed at the Dutch counsel. She explained her current predicament, and Cazeaux reacted by inviting her to spy for the Russians. Mata Hari was an unusual choice for a spy given her fame and complete inability to blend with the crowd. However, she had shared her bed with high-ranking officials on both sides of the war, and it was this intimacy that Kroemer, Ladoux, and Cazeaux hoped to exploit.

Next, Mata Hari traveled to Madrid and sent another letter to Ladoux, again refusing to use invisible ink, asking what she should do now. With no answer, she tried to carry out her mission from Madrid, making contact with German officials based there. It didn't take long for Mata Hari to procure information from powerful men. She made the acquaintance of a Major Kalle, who according to Mata Hari's accounts let slip key details about the disembarkation of a German submarine on the coast of French-controlled Morocco. Later he told her the Germans had produced a key to break the cipher used by the French in their radio communications.

Mata Hari immediately passed this information on to a Colonel Devignes, an attaché of the French embassy in Madrid. Mata Hari had a naive trust of anyone French. She wrote long, incriminating letters and handed them over to third parties, asked direct questions, and continued to demand money. Ladoux was desperate to find a way to get rid of her.

After passing on the valuable information she managed to get out of Major Kalle, Mata Hari considered her mission accomplished. It was time to return to France to collect her reward. But before she had packed her cases, she received word from Spanish Senator Emilio Junoy, warning her that the French considered her "hostile to the Allies." Furious, Mata Hari returned to Paris seeking an explanation. She thought Colonel Denvignes would sort this matter out.

Denvignes had gladly taken the information Mata Hari collected for the French and had given every indication that he was completely besotted by her. But on return to Paris, Mata Hari found that no-one would admit to knowing him. Through complicated means, Mata Hari intercepted Denvignes as he attempted to leave Paris by train and demanded to know what had happened. She believed, mistakenly, that Denvignes had gone over Ladoux's head. Instead, Denvignes had betrayed Mata Hari. It was only a matter of time before she would feel the cost of that betrayal.

Chapter Ten

The Trial and Execution of Mata Hari

"A harlot? Yes, but a traitress, never!"

—Mata Hari

Just like Denvignes, Ladoux also tried to avoid Mata Hari, but she eventually pinned him down. He claimed to have heard nothing of her triumph in Madrid; no information had been passed to him. When Mata Hari recounted that the Germans had broken the code used in French radio communications and were well aware that the French had broken their code, Ladoux acted in horror but never verified the information Mata Hari gave him. The Germans continued to use the broken code, knowing the French could intercept their messages.

Almost immediately after Mata Hari's meeting with Ladoux, messages incriminating her were transmitted using the German's broken code. Information revealed many years later showed that Ladoux himself was in all likelihood a double agent, working for the Germans, a detail that explains his treatment of Mata Hari. The messages detailed H21's (the codename Kroemer gave to Mata Hari) movements and details of funds transferred to her. Now Ladoux had the evidence he needed to arrest Mata Hari as a German spy, but he chose not to. Instead, he avoided her, refused to hand over her reward, and denied all knowledge of her mission.

Mata Hari tried to return to her life in Paris but had no money, no friends, and no lover, as she was yet to hear news of Vadim. She sensed that she had been led into a trap and was wary of what might come next. Leaving her hotel infrequently, she tried to lose the two French agents who had resumed their constant surveillance. This situation continued until around mid-January 1917 when Mata Hari finally received a visit from Vadim. He showed her a letter he had received from his commanding officer, forbidding him from seeing her. Mata Hari's name had been so thoroughly blackened by this point that to consort with her was tantamount to treachery. Yet Vadim was clearly as deeply in love with Mata Hari as she was with him; he had no intention of abandoning her.

Vadim could not, however, protect Mata Hari from her fate, and the famous dancer realized she had to leave Paris. She went to the Ministry for Foreign Affairs to get a travel permit to return to Holland on February 12, 1917. On the same day, a warrant was issued for her arrest. At the time, Mata Hari was staying at the Elysée Palace Hotel, an establishment far less elegant than what she was used to. On February 13, Police Commissioner Albert Priolet knocked on Mata Hari's hotel room door. He and four other officers entered, arrested her, and seized a number of her belongings, including any documents they could find.

Mata Hari was taken to Captain Pierre Bouchardon, a magistrate of the Third Council of War whose colleagues referred to as "the Grand Inquisitor." During Mata Hari's first meeting with Bouchardon, she was advised that she had the right to a lawyer. She refused, stating that she was innocent of any wrong-doing and that she had only acted on the instructions of French counter-espionage. Clearly, Mata Hari didn't yet realize how much trouble she was in.

Bouchardon treated Mata Hari with contempt from their very first meeting. He had her committed to Saint-Lazare prison, a notoriously filthy, damp, and strict facility. She was kept in almost total isolation, given paltry rations of food, and denied the opportunity to exercise or bathe. These conditions were unbearable for a woman who was used to the best lifestyle money could buy.

Over the coming weeks, Bouchardon subjected Mata Hari to lengthy interrogations, always finding nothing incriminating in her accounts. All of her numerous belongings were thoroughly searched, and still nothing incriminating was found amongst them. Little by little, Mata Hari recounted the specifics of her mission in Madrid. Her naivety was astounding. Ladoux had given her no way to pass on the information she had gleaned for him and found it all too easy to deny any knowledge of recruiting her for the French.

After two months of imprisonment in terrible conditions, Mata Hari's health had declined. She was coughing up blood, a common symptom of tuberculosis, and suffering from extreme anxiety. She wrote letters to Bouchardon begging him to release her, but Bouchardon had made up his mind. In his opinion, Mata Hari was a woman with no morals, a degenerate who had committed despicable acts for which she must be punished. Mata Hari's sexual promiscuity was somehow analogous with espionage in Bouchardon's mind. He only had to prove it.

Throughout this period, Vadim sent unanswered letters. On a brief return to Paris in March, he looked for Mata Hari but couldn't find her and no-one enlightened him to her plight. Mata Hari wrote a letter to the Dutch consulate in mid-March, which Bouchardon intercepted. Bouchardon knew Mata Hari's incarceration was problematic. The Dutch embassy had not been notified that one of their citizens, a neutral, was being held on serious charges with no evidence against them. Mata Hari continued writing letters to Bouchardon, pleading, begging, and arguing her innocence, but he was unmoved. The interrogations continued. The conditions worsened.

It wasn't until two whole months into the incarceration that the Dutch consulate as well as Mata Hari's loyal maid Anna and lover van der Capellan learned of her plight. By then it was too late. The first evidence of Mata Hari's treachery made a sudden appearance in late April, thanks to Georges Ladoux. Ladoux gave Bouchardon a series of incriminating telegrams sent by Kalle, the German major Mata Hari had met in Madrid. The telegrams were written in a broken code, which raised a red flag about their authenticity. However, this detail was never shared, and the telegrams were presented in their translated form.

Three months into her imprisonment, Mata Hari was broken in body and mind. It was in a state of nervous breakdown that Mata Hari finally revealed to Bouchardon that she had met with Kroemer. She insisted that she had never done anything to assist Kroemer or the war effort in general, but she had accepted money. With that confession, Mata Hari's fate was sealed.

One by one, Mata Hari's lovers denounced her, including Vadim, who claimed that their relationship was nothing more than a fling. Bouchardon insisted that Mata Hari name her accomplices. She had none and refused to incriminate an innocent person. Aware that her life was at risk, Mata Hari began to break with reality. Yet, one final letter showed she still had a little fight left to plead her case. She wrote, "That which is permitted to Mata Hari—dancer—is certainly not permitted to Madame Zelle MacLeod. That which happened to Mata Hari, these are events that do not happen to Madame Zelle. Those who address one do not address the others. In their action and their manner of living Mata Hari and Madame Zelle cannot be the same."

Yet they were the same, in body at least, and both Madame Zelle and Mata Hari went to trial on July 24, 1917. To be closer to the trial venue, Mata Hari was finally released from Saint-Lazare and moved to the Conciergerie. The prosecutor was Lieutenant André Mornet, and the seven trial judges were all high-ranking military men. Mornet called five witnesses, including Ladoux, all of whom expressed their opinion that Mata Hari was a born spy. Mornet closed his summation with the statement, "The evil that this woman has done is unbelievable. This is perhaps the greatest woman spy of the century."

Mata Hari was pronounced guilty on all charges and sentenced to death. Her possessions would be sold to pay for the cost of her trial and execution. Desperate, she put in a number of appeals against the verdict, but all were denied. On October 14, the order for her execution was made official. One day later, on October 15, 1917, Mata Hari would be put to death.

Conclusion

Mata Hari tried to prepare for her execution as she would any other night on the stage. Her wardrobe, however, left a lot to be desired. She had only the two-piece dove grey suit, low cut blouse, stockings, and hat she had worn for her trial. Her hair was grey and dirty; her skin was sallow through weight loss. Yet she pinned up her hair and pinched her cheeks, ready to meet her public.

Mata Hari's only visitors in prison, Sister Marie and Sister Léonide, accompanied her to meet the firing squad that would execute her. Dozens of people fought to catch a glimpse of Mata Hari during her last minutes on earth. "All these people," Mata Hari whispered, "What a success!"

Declining the offer of a blindfold, she stood with dignity in front of 12 soldiers from the 23rd Dragoons. Defiantly, she blew a kiss to the men. The sergeant major gave the order and the soldiers fired, sending several bullets into Mata Hari's body. Her life was taken by a close-range shot to the head.

Years after Mata Hari's execution, the men who sentenced her to death admitted the evidence against her was flimsy at best. With no evidence of actual espionage, she was judged because of her perceived immorality and paid the ultimate price. In the eyes of her persecutors, Mata Hari had no shame. They could not grasp that she had been formed in a completely different world to wartime France. A European celebrity of the Belle

Époque, Mata Hari lived a life of glamor and sensuality and made no apologies for how she earned her wage. She knew no other way—and had no other way—to survive.

Remembered today as the quintessential *femme fatale*, Mata Hari will be forever young. Unjustly executed, she can be seen in contemporary times as a martyr to female liberation who lived only for herself. And yet, Mata Hari was capable of love. Had things turned out differently who knows what the future held for Mata Hari and her beloved Vadim. As Rudolf, Mata Hari's brutish ex-husband, said upon hearing the news of her execution, "Whatever she's done in life, she did not deserve that."

Made in the USA
Middletown, DE
14 April 2020